*The Juggle is Real*

*The Juggle is Real: Finding success and balance as a mompreneur*

Copyright © 2022 by Bethany Meadows
All rights reserved. This book or any portion thereof may not be reproduced or used in any manner whatsoever without the express written permission of the publisher except for the use of brief quotations in a book review.

Cover design: Anthony Guin
Cover image: Getty Images, www.istockphoto.com
Interior layout by: Anthony Guin
Edited by: Ann Marie Harvey / Jenny Waltman
Printed in the United States of America

First Printing, 2022
ISBN: 9798360447351
Imprint: Independently published

For questions or to request copies, please contact:
Vertical Solutions Media
5637 Myron Clark Rd
McCalla AL 35111

# *Dedication*

Thanks always to my husband, Jeff. You may not always understand my crazy, but I'm thankful you decide to run with it anyway. You keep me steady and grounded, and we both know it's not an easy job.

Thank you to my amazing kids. You encourage and cheer me on exactly when I need it most. Now that you're grown up, my greatest blessing is your friendship.

And, of course, thank you to the tribe of women who inspire, encourage and kick me in the pants. I don't know where I'd be without you!

*The Juggle is Real*

# TABLE OF CONTENTS

*Introduction*   7

*Chapter 1:*
Being a mom AND a business owner is challenging.   13

*Chapter 2:*
What is your version of work-life balance?   23

*Chapter 3:*
Get clear on your WHY.   31

*Chapter 4:*
Grab hold of your big girl panties
(and understand your strengths).   37

*Chapter 5:*
Skills for life and business.   49

*Chapter 6:*
Leadership qualities of a successful mompreneur.   65

*Chapter 7:*
A successful business starts with a powerful brand.   73

*Chapter 8:*
Smoothing out friction.   91

*Chapter 9:*
Establishing parenting objectives.   99

*Chapter 10:*
Creating a custom parenting plan.   107

*Chapter 11:*
Building a tribe.   117

*The Juggle is Real*

*Introduction*

The growth of women business owners over the past decade is staggering. In 2010, the percentage of small businesses owned by women was just 29%. Today, the number has skyrocketed to more than four of every 10 businesses. In 2021, 1,821 new female-owned business were started every single day!*

It's a great time to be a woman in business. And as an entrepreneur, you passionately work to get your start-up off the ground. You embrace competition with a determined grin. You stare down an unpredictable marketplace knowing you are flexible enough to evolve as needed. You are a rockstar entrepreneur.

Now, if you happen to be a business owner who is also called mom, taxi driver, chef extraordinaire, personal shopper, boo-boo fixer, snack maker and the other 4,367 roles you fill every day for your family…you, my friend, are a mega rockstar mompreneur!

**The typical mompreneur is like a duck.**

On the surface of the water, we are so calm and put together. We glide around chatting with the other ducks wearing our overwhelm like a weird badge of honor. We even hint that we *might* actually make it to the gym later with a slight chuckle. Our little ducklings follow behind in a nice single file line…with matching hair bows (private joke – you'll get it later).

But under the surface, our feet are paddling frantically, we swim mostly in circles and the sweet ducklings are squawking at each other on the way to the pond. And we already know the gym isn't happening because self-care is the first thing we sacrifice when we exceed the margins of our time and bandwidth.

**This book is for mompreneurs ready for success AND balance.**

As a mompreneur, you are juggling *all the things* in business AND in motherhood. As you add more things to either side, you juggle faster. After all, you are a confident capable woman and you are certain you can do it all. You are going to do it all whatever it takes.

But maybe you're also…

A mompreneur who feels guilty about the time you spend working in your business…

A mompreneur who is tired and burned out from trying

# INTRODUCTION

to do it all…

A mompreneur who is ready for your business to grow to the next level…

A mompreneur who has chased work/life balance right into the abyss of overwhelm…

A mompreneur who wants to create processes and learn strategies for creating a more balanced life…

Girl, this book is for you.

**Why did I write this book?**

I have been a mompreneur for almost 20 years. I started my second business in 2008 as a single mom homeschooling five children. I know all too well how exhausting it is to try and do it all. I'm pretty sure in a period of about five years I got five hours sleep…like in total. They should have done a sleep study on me to figure out how I was still alive.

I felt alone and isolated during this time in my life. I believed no one understood my choices and I often felt judged. Taking time for myself in any way felt selfish. I chased business success with a mindset of scarcity and the fear of not making enough or being enough to succeed. My insecurity resulted in pricing my services based on what I thought others could afford, rather than my own worth.

Personal development, mindset, self-care and community were all foreign concepts.

My journey toward success and balance is ongoing. In fact, I do not expect to "arrive" any time soon…or ever. My definitions of success and balance are always evolving based on my circumstances.

**This is what I will share in this book.**

Being a mompreneur is challenging. But AMAZING!
I love my business. I'm passionate about the work I do with business owners and entrepreneurs. I also love being a mom and Nana. My family is one of my greatest joys. "Figuring out" how to be the best version of me in both roles has always been my ideal. I want to share what worked for me.

Personally, I love the practical and tactical. I will share actionable strategies you can use to find your ideal balance between business and family.

We will discuss how to find clarity on your "why." Clarity of purpose is key, especially when the naysayers decide they know what is better for your family than you do. Your "why" will keep you focused on your goals and what truly matters to you.

Imagine the power of identifying a limiting belief and removing it from your life! I'm going to share some strategies for learning how to overcome limiting beliefs. It will be a complete game changer for your business and your personal life. A major key to success is mindset, then action.

We are going to dig into key skills which changed my world for the better. How to battle imposter syndrome, brainstorming and the skill of planning will be part of our focus. We are going to discuss mompreneur leadership and how to move your influence to the next level. We are going to learn how to identify friction and create strategies to remove them from our lives and business. We will focus on building a community for encouragement, support and creative opportunities.

I'm going to teach how to create a powerful brand for business which will drive success. You will learn how to create a touchpoint map for elevating a customer's brand experience and turn them into raving fans.

Finally, we'll dig into being intentional as a parent by establishing objectives and creating a supportive parenting plan. I'm going to share my secret weapon to never again finding yourself in a fruitless argument with a toddler or teen. A bold claim…but I promise you, it works.

Does that sound worthwhile to you? If so, let's get started!

*Source: earthweb.com*

*The Juggle is Real*

*Chapter 1*

# Being a mom AND a business owner is challenging.

Forgive me for sounding terrible. As a career mom of an only child, I sincerely believed anyone with more than one child was crazy. How judgmental! Let me explain.

I was a tired working mama of a toddler. The 90-minute one-way commute was long and tedious. My job was demanding. The person I depended upon for support was a raging alcoholic. Most days being a mom meant focusing on survival. As in, "Hey! My daughter's in one piece! Go me!"

I married at 19 and became a mom a few months shy of my 21st birthday. I traveled out of the country to visit my in-laws and surprise, gave birth almost seven weeks early. So much for the doctor I knew and trusted. So much for all those Lamaze classes. My baby girl decided it was time, so it was time.

In looking back on those years through the lens of experience, it's a wonder I made it. Days blurred together.

A haze of being up before the sun, arriving at the daycare at 6:30 a.m., to be at my job by 8:00 a.m. After working all day, I reworked the pattern in reverse, arriving home at 7:00 p.m. to cook dinner, give my baby a bath, collapse into bed and prepare myself to do the ritual all over again.

Weekdays left no room for anything other than work, caring for my baby and getting to bed. Everything else had to be crammed into the weekends. Add in a husband with an alcohol addiction and I was one stressed-out young mama.

Many days I questioned whether I was being a good mom. I wiped away tears as I left my precious girl in the care of others. I beat myself up with accusations of selfishness and inadequacy. When she cut her finger on a toy, I felt the weight of the injury believing I did not keep her safe. She wore her rain boots to daycare because I was too tired to argue with a toddler—and was immediately chastised for not putting her tennis shoes on (they were in her backpack, but whatever, Karen). My mother-in-law criticized the clothes I chose for her. The negative feedback came from all sides—confirming all the ways I was not enough.

If you're reading this book, you may relate to the feelings I experienced. Perhaps you often find yourself overwhelmed from the weight of "all the things." Being a mom is amazing and one of the best gifts in our lives. Motherhood is also one of the most challenging. Being an entrepreneur is also amazing. And, like motherhood, it's super-duper challenging. Add the two aspects of our lives together and you have the makings of a mompreneur—part superhero,

Being a mom AND a business owner is challenging.

part ready to crawl in a hole and die, because at least when you are dead you can sleep.

---

I always wanted to own my own business. By the time I was nine, I started Bethany's Roadrunner Service. I posted flyers featuring a hand-drawn roadrunner (inspired by Looney Tunes, of course) around our condominium building to advertise my errand services for elderly residents. When I was 11, I accepted an early morning newspaper route, delivering roughly 300 papers before 7:00 a.m. daily.

My early childhood experiences as a young entrepreneur taught me several valuable lessons. The harder you work, the more money you make. And, sometimes customers are stupid butt faces, but you can't tell them that—even if you really want to—at least not to their face.

My entrepreneurial journey took a backseat for about a decade when I married and had a baby. I took a job at an insurance company as a receptionist in a branch office. Dreams of running my own business were on hold due to all the "reasons" I perceived as barriers. Too young, I have a baby, a difficult situation at home, financial challenges, not enough education, not enough time, etc. I was in the corporate world now, and for the next 10 years I focused on climbing the next rung on the ladder.

Those 10 years were formative. I embraced the corporate "game" and played it well. I measured success by the size of my office, performance reviews and my paycheck. My happiest moment of the day (and most guilt-ridden moment) was picking up my daughter from daycare or school. Nothing beats a child who lights up when she sees you and runs excitedly into your arms. Those were the best hugs anyone could imagine. I found myself comfortable in my corporate career.

---

The day started as any other. Coffee and chitchat in the break room. Organizing my desk and tasks for the day. When we were all called to the conference room, I felt something in the air.

Our company was merging with another larger company. They didn't want our division and was selling our block of business to a competitor. Our management team saw an opportunity to create their own small company by obtaining a contract to manage our existing block of business.

I was offered a place in this new company as an employee, but I no longer wanted to play that part. The management team was excited about their new company-leased Jeep Cherokees. They chatted incessantly about the opportunity to be business owners. I remembered my long-forgotten passion to own my own business. I felt a shift which caused a discontent with the 9 to 5.

When word began to spread about the merger, I was "headhunted" by competitors. I found myself being flown around the country for interviews and wooed with opportunities. In my heart, it felt like more of the same corporate journey, and I couldn't get excited. The owner of

BEING A MOM AND A BUSINESS OWNER IS CHALLENGING.

one of the third-party administrator companies I worked with heard the news. He offered me the chance to start a company with him. He would finance it and I would run it. We would be equal partners. Um…I'm going with YES!

The entrepreneurial spirit is a funny thing. A person is willing to work 80 hours a week to be paid for 40 (or 20)? Being in control of your destiny has a pretty powerful pull. Having an idea and the freedom to implement it is exhilarating. Investing in future returns excites and inspires. The flexibility to volunteer at my daughter's school and go on field trips was another win. I had found the very definition of "living your best life."

After three years of partnership, my partner elected to go a different direction. I purchased his share of the business and continued as the sole owner.

**Running a business full-time while raising a child is hard. Doing it while homeschooling is even harder.**

At first, the decision to homeschool came because I felt backed into a corner. We had moved and the new school system was atrocious. In the 10 days my daughter was enrolled, she was bullied physically and emotionally. On day 10, she witnessed a classmate break another student's nose by grabbing hair and slamming a face into a desk. Blood exploded everywhere, kids were screaming and she was traumatized. The next day I called the school with an excuse she was sick. The day after, I unenrolled her.

I didn't want to homeschool. I didn't believe I was

*Comparing the best moments of others with our worst moments robs us of our joy. Be the opposite of Nike and "just don't do it."*

qualified or capable. In fact, doing homework with my daughter was nothing more than a power play between her and me. I was convinced homeschooling would be all that times ten. The private schools were full, so my options were homeschooling or taking her to self-defense classes. I decided I would homeschool her for the rest of the school year and started looking into self-defense classes…just in case. The day six boxes of homeschool curriculum arrived at my doorstep, I broke down crying. What made me think I could do this?

Long story short, homeschooling ended up being a beautiful gift. We both excelled and thrived. She never attended a traditional school again until college.

**Running a business full-time while homeschooling a child is hard. Doing it while homeschooling FIVE children is even harder.**

My adoption story is long and irrelevant to this book. What's important to know is we added a sibling group of

BEING A MOM AND A BUSINESS OWNER IS CHALLENGING.

four children ages 8, 9, 10 and 11. The last thing I ever saw myself doing was adopting four children, and like homeschooling, I felt ill-equipped and set up for failure.

I often heard from others observing my family and business you are a "saint" or a "supermom." I knew better. I was nowhere even close to either. I asked God through my tears "why me?" on a regular basis.

Many times I wondered if I was ruining my kids. The questions were ongoing like a broken soundtrack. Would I ever have a normal life again where all the little people did not hate me? Would there be a time when smelly laundry did not take over my house? Would I ever have the time to grow my business beyond chasing the mortgage payment every month?

---

This is a good moment for a reminder: comparison is a thief. We look at others at church or our kid's school, or worse, on social media, and we think "they" have it all together. "They" make it look easy or "they" are doing "all the things" better. We second-guess our parenting decisions; we doubt our abilities to lead our businesses. Comparing the best moments of others with our worst moments robs us of our joy. Be the opposite of Nike and "just don't do it."

---

After several years of adjusting to the new family dynamic, we began to find our groove. Ultimately, I sold the business to give 100 percent of my time and focus to homeschooling. Raising my five beautiful children became my passion.

## The Juggle is Real

**Running a business while homeschooling five children is hard. Doing it as a sole breadwinner and single mom is the hardest thing I've ever done.**

I've never been slammed in the face with a piece of lumber. When I discovered my husband's relationship with another woman a two-by-four slamming me in the face felt like a good description. The resulting divorce knocked me down for a minute. Okay, no lies here, more than a minute. The affair was a massive shock. I found myself scrambling to pick up the pieces to understand what life would now look like. My hair fell out in handfuls. I lost weight, and not in the "Yay, I lost weight!" kind of way. More in the "Dang, girl, are you sick?" kind of way. I put on a fake face for all but a few, and pretended to be okay. I was anything but okay. I was broken and sad.

As you might expect, the kids were devastated when their dad left. Betrayal and abandonment hit them as much as it did me. They needed me to be okay and I tried to be. I hung onto my faith in God with the kind of death grip strength one deploys on the outside turn while water tubing behind a speed boat. A grip coming from the knowledge letting go will be more painful than hanging on. I hung on. "Staying vertical" became my new motto. I added it to my screen saver, phone background, wrote it on the bathroom mirror and anywhere else I could think of. I needed the reminder every single day—I still do.

Being a mom AND a business owner is challenging.

**Being a mompreneur may be the hardest thing you ever do, but it will be worth it.**

Everyone has a story. I have a story. You have a story. We have all met and overcome obstacles. We have kicked down barriers to success. We've stared down challenges with an evil eye perfected by motherhood.

Now you find yourself reading this book. I imagine it's because you're the kind of business mama rock star who knows continuous improvement is a required element of success. Maybe, just maybe, you *like* to dig in and learn new ways to do more with less. Well, perfect! Me too!

Running a business and managing a home and family takes hard work, grit, determination and a collection of SKILLS we can implement.

I'm excited to drill down on skills, strategies and mindsets to set you up for success, both in business and as a mom. Long days and constantly shifting gears can leave you drained in every sense of the word. You CAN build a framework of systems and processes to streamline key aspects of your life and business—so you can breathe again.

I'm so glad you are here and I'm excited to take this journey with you!

*The Juggle is Real*

*Chapter 2*

# What is your version of work-life balance?

Work-life balance is the ultimate oxymoron. It's a fantasy world where we have time for everything, where nothing ever goes sideways. In our utopia, the people in our world are happy and content, including ourselves. When it happens, the magical moment lasts for about 3.8 seconds.

I spent my formative years in a culture where I was taught that women could have it all. For a while I believed it and strived hard to make it happen. When you believe a goal is achievable, yet are unable to make it happen, inadequacy hits hard. You perceive others as attaining the sweet spot, so you "must" be doing it wrong. The result? You push even harder…or you quit.

Then life does what life does—it happens. Divorce, a sick child, a financial crisis. Now the so-called work-life balance runs off a cliff and bursts into flames. You decide to view the crisis as a season in time, which it is, and double down. You are a supermom…after all. You tackle the next issue and the next because we're supposed to turn all problems into opportunities. Right?

I realized after my divorce was finalized that I was burned out. I was working long hours on my business. I was homeschooling children up to 10 hours a day. The clock in the kitchen said 7:00 p.m. and I had not even thought about dinner. The very idea of cooking dinner made me want to cry. I was so exhausted that walking and talking required a lot of intentional effort. I asked the kids if they wouldn't mind eating cereal for dinner…again. It was more of a statement "eat cereal for dinner" than a question. I walked into my bedroom and collapsed on the bed fully clothed and slept for 12 hours. I was DONE in every way a person can be done. And "dang it" if I still don't feel a twinge of guilt over not being enough in those moments.

Maybe you have never been burned out to such a degree. Maybe it shows up for you as a constant buzzing in the back of your head. It nags at your failures. It attacks your worth when you say no to something because you don't have enough time to fit it in. Maybe you are chasing the mirage of work-life balance and hope you will get there. You keep telling yourself to work harder, smarter, faster.

Want to know what no one tells you about work-life balance? Your interpretation of the ideal work-life balance is different from everyone else's version. Yep, that's right. *You get to* decide what the balance looks like for you and your family. Your world is uniquely yours. You have different demands on your time and energy. You have different values and priorities. Your life looks different from mine.

A few encouragements to remember when establishing the right work-life balance for you:

1) **Decide on the activities which create the right dynamic for your world.** Don't try to compare or copy others around you, on social media, in the movies or the neighbors next door. Figure out what serves you well and include in your life. If it's not serving you well, remove it from your life.

Don't be fooled by the simplicity. Choices will be tested by your emotions of the moment, your best friend's opinion and even your own family. Write down and identify how and why the activities your family plans to do serve you best. Your list will provide a strong conviction and clarity when you need to say, "Sorry, that's not a good fit for us right now."

2) **Work-life balance is not sliced up like a pie.** You probably are familiar with the ol' pie chart where you identify the different parts of work and life. Then give each area a certain size slice to represent the time we assign to each piece. For real...when was the last time you stopped and considered whether your choices fit into the slice of pie you created? Me either. Forget the pie. The pie is gone. Somebody ate it.

The problem with the pie chart is it does not account for the ever-changing, evolving world called life. Things do not fit neatly inside a slice. When you "plan" your work-life balance around a predetermined sized slice, you are going

*Choose what truly matters, draw your line in the sand and give yourself a heaping pile of grace.*

to feel like you are failing. Because in mompreneur world, nothing, or almost nothing, goes as planned. Pie charts are not flexible, but we need to be.

3) **You don't have to do everything yourself.** The supermom complex is real. But you are not a martyr. You are an intelligent, confident and capable woman and as such, you *can* allow others to help you. In fact, you should master the skill of delegation and wield it regularly.

As a business leader, you should delegate everything someone else can do. Accept the fact that things may only be done 80 percent as well as if you had done them yourself. READ THAT AGAIN. Absorb it. Accept it. Then celebrate because having it completed is better than not done at all.

The same strategy applies at home. Your children are capable of doing far more than they will volunteer to do. I know, shocking! Assigning them meaningful responsibilities will help create more margin in your life. Plus, empowering their contribution will teach them work ethic and increase their self-esteem. Helping you helps them. It's a win-win.

4) **Achieving work-life balance is not the destination.** Are you familiar with the phrase, "it's about the journey, not the destination?" Work-life balance is kind of like the destination—the place we never find but are always trying to go. Once we embrace the journey instead, we can find contentment in the path. The goal is progress, not perfection. Give yourself a break. Remember doing your best, in the moment, is enough. In fact, giving your best is more than enough. You <u>are</u> enough.

5) **It's important to factor in margin.** If you run at full capacity all the time, an unexpected or unplanned event will send you into a spiral. Picture a circle in your mind. The lines of the circle are you at 100% capacity. Now draw another circle about 20% toward the center inside that first circle. This circle is your "ideal" and where you will best run on a day-to-day basis. If something unexpected happens, you will have the margin to expand. Factoring in margin requires reducing the addition of more and more to your work and life! *Looking at you, sis.* If you keep saying yes, you will no longer have any margin. If the goal is balance, margin is required.

6) **Forget time management and embrace energy management.** We only have so much time and managing time doesn't provide any more for us to use. However, our energy has a massive impact on what we can get done in a day. To learn how to manage our energy, we must understand our natural cadences and what affects us. Sleep,

diet, relationship with a spouse, traffic, kids making us late, mid-afternoon sugar crash, annoying clients, the latest project, et cetera, et cetera, all impact energy. Some energy drainers are outside our control. We can manage our energy by proactively protecting or adjusting our responses. If nothing else, write on a sticky note as a daily reminder to "Protect your energy."

7) **Work-life balance includes taking care of you.** When you get on a plane, the flight attendants do a safety demonstration. They always instruct you to put your mask on FIRST, then on the child next to you. The supermom complex leads us to feel responsible for everyone and everything. Saving the world is noble, but if we go down in a ball of flaming glory, we are no good to anyone. For years I believed I had to "sacrifice" myself to take care of my family. What a load of shiitake mushrooms! Think about what renews your energy and makes you feel recharged. Be intentional about including those things in your life. Have fun. If you plan something super crazy, call me. I'm in.

8) **Every day is a new day.** We all have days which simply suck. That is life, and sometimes life does not go as planned. Sometimes we bark at the kids, yell at the dog or give our husbands the stare of a thousand deaths, causing him to take refuge in the garage. Listen up, sister. We've all been there, done that. If you have a bad day, give yourself grace. You are not a horrible mom or wife or boss. You are human. Go apologize to whomever you terrorized yesterday or today

and move on.

Bottom line, you can do all the planning and scheduling of a woman on a mission, but *you can't control everything*. Living stressed, overwhelmed and/or burned out is no way to live. Choose what truly matters, draw your line in the sand and give yourself a heaping pile of grace.

Life's too short not to live with joy inside your margin.

*The Juggle is Real*

*Chapter 3*

# Get clear on your WHY

When you are a mom, there are always people who think they know what's best for you and your children. As a single mom homeschooling five children, I heard, "Why don't you just put them in school?" "Why don't you get a real job?" Ugh! If I only had a quarter for all the unnecessary questions or well-meaning advice.

It's super annoying when people presume to know better. If I had not been clear on my WHY, those questions might have derailed my focus and determination. What the naysayers didn't understand was my purpose transcended what they saw as the easier or more logical path.

Getting clear on your WHY gives you clarity so when things get hard, you have a reason to dig in and stick it out. Your WHY rises above the temporary obstacles or annoyances. Your WHY'S purpose is long-lasting and has greater impact than anything you will deal with on a given

*The WHY is unique to each life and business. When the juggle gets real, WHY is a guiding focus.*

day. Your WHY becomes the compass by which you set your course.

Your business needs a WHY as part of its brand identity. There are hard days in business. Your WHY is a narrative extending beyond revenue and becomes a part of your unique value proposition. You will attract customers who share the values of your business WHY.

Your WHY helps you prioritize, make decisions about product, future hires and more. WHY is the filter through which you determine what aligns with your mission.

There are three strategies you can use to help determine your WHY. I recommend doing each strategy to reveal a deeper sense of your WHY.

**Your Life WHY**

What does "living your best life" mean to you? Determining your life's WHY helps you decide if you need to make changes to get back on track.

**First,**

Answer the following questions:

- What inspired the decision to have children?
- What is interesting about my family's story?
- What is unique about my family?
- What are my parenting objectives? What characteristics do I want my children to have as adults?
- What morals and values do I hold dear?

**Then,**

Find your purpose by:

- Determine your top five core family values.
- What do I want my family to be remembered for when I am gone?
- What family goals matter most?
- Is my purpose aspirational?
- Does my purpose evolve as my goals and values change?

At this point, what does your WHY look like? Do you have an idea? Take it deeper with the last strategy.

**Finally,**

Determine the benefits:

- State the proposed purpose.
- What's the benefit of that?
- What's the benefit of that?
- What's the benefit of that?

- What's the benefit of that?
- Restate the proposed purpose.

When people challenged my decisions, it caused me to doubt and second-guess myself. Making good choices for my kids was important and I wanted to get it right. Getting clear on my WHY helped give me clarity and confidence about my decision which prevented me from getting swayed by other voices and allowed me to stand strong on my purpose.

The following shows how this last step can really get to a deeper sense of your WHY.

**Stated purpose**: I'm homeschooling while running a business as a single mom because it is what is best for my kids.

**What's the benefit of that?** They get more focused one-on-one attention customized to their needs.

**What's the benefit of that?** They are able to learn more quickly in an emotionally safe environment.

**What's the benefit of that?** They become more confident in their abilities to learn and to love who they are.

**What's the benefit of that?** They see themselves as contributors to the world, rather than just existing in the world.

**Restate the purpose.** I'm homeschooling while running a business as a single mom because I'm breaking a generational curse. I am raising children to be world changers and influencers.

Can you see how getting clear on your WHY provides clarity? The process above took my purpose from "what's best for them" to "how they will impact the world." The heightened sense of purpose is what will drive you forward when things get difficult.

**Your business WHY.**
Determining your business WHY is crafted using the same process.

**First,**
Answer the following questions:

- What inspired my business idea?
- What is interesting about my founding story?
- What is unique about my business?
- What are the problems I am trying to solve?
- What do I believe in, both professionally and personally?

**Then,**
Find your purpose by:

- Determine the top five core values.
- What do I want my company to be known for even after I'm gone?
- What goals of my company matter most?
- Does my purpose transcend revenue? Is it aspirational?
- Does it evolve as my goals and values change?

**Finally,**

Determine the benefits:

- State the proposed purpose.
- What's the benefit of that?
- What's the benefit of that?
- What's the benefit of that?
- What's the benefit of that?
- Restate the proposed purpose.

The WHY is unique to each life and business. When the juggle gets real, WHY is a guiding focus.

It's important to review the WHY on occasion to ensure the answer continues to make sense for the situation. Our lives and business will evolve and grow. Our WHY needs to keep evolving and growing with us.

*Chapter 4*

# Grab hold of your big girl panties (and understand your strengths)

I've always liked the phrase "grab hold of your big girl panties." Appealing to my sense of independence and my toddler self, I continue to insist I can do it myself. My mom is fond of telling the story of my first day in kindergarten. She doesn't share how cute I was or how excited I was to learn. Instead, the story is about an obnoxious and bossy five-year-old telling the other kids to sit down and be quiet. Although cringeworthy, I have to give props to my younger self's confident swagger.

The way we are raised, our experiences and the people who influenced us leave impressions. As we grow older, those impressions are internalized into what we believe about ourselves. When the internal beliefs are negative, they can hold us back.

Here's the thing—we don't always realize we have limiting beliefs. We aren't looking for them. We see our

*Don't waste time in your comfort zone. Kick fear in the teeth and embrace living out your purpose.*

beliefs as part of our personality and how we are wired.

My dad was a bit larger than life and could be quite intimidating. He was quick to criticize and slow to praise. I learned from a young age I would have to work hard to earn his approval.

As an adult, my internalized beliefs showed up as perfectionism and workaholism. From my perspective it was "just the way I am." If I'm being honest, I thought the way I worked was a positive trait and I was proud of these attributes.

As I grew into a better sense of myself, I realized I had internalized a devastating limiting belief. *I would never be more than average at best. Even on my best day, I'd never be enough for true success. I do not deserve success. I would have to work harder than everyone else to be like most people. Rising above was not within my grasp. I will never be enough.*

Can you see how my belief caused fear and hesitation to reach for greatness?

What about you? Do you have a quality you have accepted as a part of your personality which is a limiting belief?

Consider what would happen if you identified a limiting belief and removed it from your life.

What if you could be free of what is holding you back from extraordinary success?

What would your life look like without hesitation, fear or inaction?

What if, indeed.

**Here's a list of 10 common limiting beliefs. Do any of these resonate with you?**

1. Fear of success
2. Fear of failure
3. Fear you are not good enough to achieve what you want
4. Fear of not being loved or interpreted as unlovable
5. Fear of rejection (shows up as avoiding relationships or people pleasing)
6. Negative attitude toward being rich or having money
7. Fear of greatness
8. Belief you don't deserve or are not worthy of success
9. Believing you must work very hard and long hours for your money
10. Others are to blame for holding you back

I've had all 10 of these limiting beliefs plague me at one time or another, and I'm still working on many of them.

Limiting beliefs hold us back from being who we were created to be, diminishing our ability to live out our purpose. If we accept these limiting beliefs as a part of who we are, we will never rise to our full potential.

One of the most impactful things we can do is identify those beliefs which are holding us back. Then make a way to a different way of thinking about ourselves, the world and our place in it.

**IDENTIFY your limiting beliefs.** You've heard it said before, "The first step in fixing any problem is identifying there is a problem." Until you can speak truth about yourself, you are operating on the faulty premise that you don't need to change. That kind of thinking will keep you from being the best business leader and mom you can be. The more honest you get about yourself, the more ready you will be to move from ordinary to extraordinary.

**ACCEPT responsibility for change.** As a good mom, you insist your children accept responsibility for their actions. You do the crime; you do the time. Am I right? Why would we not hold ourselves to the same standard? The limiting beliefs you have identified have no place in your life. They need to go! It's time to make the necessary changes, no matter how uncomfortable they make you feel.

**LIVE without fear.** Tony Robbins describes certainty as a dream killer. Wow, how true! [brain bomb!] If a bird stays in the certainty of the nest, it will never learn to fly. Clinging to certainty is often driven by some sort of fear. Fear of the unknown. Fear of what "could" happen. Fear of success. Fear of failure. Life is too short to allow fear of any kind to keep us from our goals and dreams.

One of my favorite scripture verses is 2 Timothy 1:7. "For God has not given us a spirit of fear, but of **power** and of **love** and of a **sound mind**." Boom! There's a mic drop if I have ever heard one.

Ever think about how you would live differently if you knew you only had five years left to live? You'd likely hit the bucket list and take every opportunity to experience all the things. Don't waste time in your comfort zone. Kick fear in the teeth and embrace living out your purpose.

**TELL your negative inner voice to shut up.** There is a video making the rounds on social media. A little girl is standing on the bathroom counter. She is holding a hairbrush and giving herself an enthusiastic pep talk in the mirror. Cutest. Thing. Ever.

As women we tend to be hard on ourselves, but what if we chose instead to be our biggest cheerleader. When we make a mistake, we could train the voice in our heads to give us a pep talk instead of tearing ourselves down. Just as we speak life over our children, we can speak life over ourselves.

Aren't there are enough negative messages out there trying to convince us we are a victim? Telling us we are not enough? That we do not deserve anything good? My sweet friends, grab your hairbrush, find the nearest mirror and repeat after me:

*"I AM fearfully and wonderfully made. I AM worth prioritizing. I WAS CREATED for a unique purpose. I WILL make a difference with my choices. My children ARE BLESSED because I am their mother. My business WILL SUCCEED. I REJECT all limiting beliefs keeping me from living out my purpose."*

**Success requires mindset FIRST and then action.**
You know the feeling you get when you listen to an inspirational speaker? They share their overcoming story, challenge you and convict you to take some sort of action. You leave the event pumped up and "motivated," but soon your good intentions are forgotten.

Ugh! It's frustrating to be at a place of excitement about the potential of something good. Then life happens, distraction happens, laziness happens—and then nothing happens. Or worse, negative inner voices pop in for an unwanted visit and remind us of what a loser we are because we <u>never</u> DO anything.

I hate running with all my being. It's boring and painful all at once. You know the round window stickers runners put on the back of cars (13.1 or 26.2) to show they have run a half or full marathon? My husband gave me one that says 0.0. The sticker says it all. Can I run? Yes. If there is a grizzly bear wanting to make me his dinner, darn right I can run. I will outrun you because the slowest runner is a meal (Sorry, sis. It's not personal).

For me to become "a runner," I would need a huge pile of mindset adjustments. Like a massive pile. My inner voice would have to work overtime convincing me I could, in fact, be a runner. I'd have to push past the fear of others thinking I look like a crazed prison escapee (hmmm, note to self: never wear orange while running). And, once my mindset shifted, I'd need to start.

If I go for a run without the mindset to back it up, it will be a short run. Maybe the end of the driveway because that's where I'll start thinking I have lost my mind. I'm not a runner. I'm already out of breath. My legs are already tired. Why did I think I could be a runner again?

You see where I'm going, don't you? How many times have we resigned ourselves to the 0.0 sticker when we really desired to achieve the 26.2 sticker?

> Mindset without action is merely a thought.
> A thought without mindset will rarely be achieved.

**Focus on the right actions.**
If you're anything like me, your brain goes a hundred miles per hour in many different directions. You are chasing squirrels and shiny objects. A sufferer of "too many ideas and so little time" syndrome. The problem with not defining right actions is you end up frantic with busy things. Then you either don't finish projects or have too many going at one time.

The Pareto Principle is also known as the 80/20 rule. 20 percent of what we do will produce 80 percent of the results. Now, I haven't actually tested this theory by tracking all the things because, you know, I have a life. However, it sure has that ring of truth.

# *A thought without mindset will rarely be achieved.*

Narrowing your focus to right actions requires you to be intentional. Here is a simple four-step process for determining the right actions to focus on.

1. What's the goal? Start with the result you want. What's your objective?
2. What resources and/or people do you need to accomplish the goal?
3. Check your mindset. Determine the inner voice you need.
4. Take action and make it happen!

**Small actions add up.**
My husband is diligent about working out, but he's busy and can't always make it to the gym. He has a habit of performing 20 body exercises as he goes about his day at the office. Waiting for his coffee cup to fill up? 20 squats. Something taking a minute to print? 20 push-ups. A call puts him on hold? 20 sit-ups. The crazy part is by the end of the day, he's done an entire workout! Small actions add up and yield results.

How much time do we waste on things that do not matter or fail to move us a step forward toward our goals?

- What if we replaced a few minutes of social media with writing 500 words for a book?
- What if we replaced a few minutes of TV with learning a new skill on YouTube?
- What if we replaced a few minutes of jamming to music in the carpool line with listening to a podcast?
- What if all these small actions led us closer to our goals?

I recently had a guest on my podcast who had some amazing strategies around productivity. One of those strategies was called "Last Day Before Vacation." Blaine Oelkers (www.selfluence.com) explained it this way: "On the last day before vacation we tend to be hyper focused because we know time is limited. We prioritize things that HAVE to get done, delegate what we can't accomplish and then leave the rest for when we get back." His challenge? What if we operated EVERY DAY like it was the last day before vacation? Brilliant!

*You can listen to the entire episode at Time to Thrive – Marketing Strategies for Small Business episode #40.*

**Be clear on what matters to you.**
One of our challenges as a mompreneur are people who think you have a "flexible" schedule. If you are not clear, let me help you out. You do not. At least not in the way they want you to be.

Being a business owner, being a mom and being all the

*Remember, if you say "yes" to something, it means you are saying "no" to something else. Before saying yes, make sure you are making a fair trade.*

other things means you are busy. <u>Your time is valuable and finite</u>. Don't give it to people who don't respect its value. It's ok to say no – firmly and often. Smile, thank them for the opportunity and say, "I don't have the bandwidth right now." If you are uncomfortable saying no to others, grab the hairbrush again and practice saying "no" in the mirror.

Remember, if you say "yes" to something, it means you are saying "no" to something else. Before saying yes, make sure you are making a fair trade.

**Set boundaries with vampires.**
The entire mission of a vampire is to suck the life right out of you. They mesmerize you with their eyes, so you are helpless when they clamp down on your neck to feed. You have vampires in your life, and you don't have to allow them, because you, my friend, are not a victim.

Vampires show up in different ways—a toxic relationship, a client who demands more than what they've paid, the list goes on. Vampires love drama, chaos and creating situations to usurp attention. Vampires must be addressed or they can destroy your peace and your path to success in both life and business.

In a later chapter we'll talk more about how to create boundaries for kids. Right now, let's talk about that client. You know the one calling at all hours. The one who is quick to complain or revises things over and over. The one who makes you question your WHY on a regular basis. Yes, that's the one.

**FIRE THEM.**

I'm not joking. Those vampires are not your ideal customer. They are a leech on your time, energy and focus. They need to go as soon as you can swing it. Bye-bye. Adios. Au revoir. Kill them with a stake and don't look back. And carry garlic with you from now on.

*The Juggle is Real*

*Chapter 5*

# Skills for life and business

Certain skills add value to your life and business—and they might not be what you're thinking. These are the skills that can be applied and used in almost every situation.

## SKILL #1 - LEARN HOW TO LEARN

Knowing how to learn is a skill that can be learned. (Ha! Say that eight times fast.) There are many ways to learn through books, podcasts, forums, courses, YouTube videos and more. If you wanted, you could get the equivalent of a Ph.D. using your keyboard and the Internet. And don't get me started on Google! There are so many answers to questions we don't even know about yet. **As the business owner, you are the ceiling for your business**. The business will never scale or grow past your skills and knowledge. As a mom, you want to model this focus and encourage your kids to follow your example.

## *Learning is your most powerful weapon against imposter syndrome.*

Lifestyle learning is the ultimate "teach a man to fish" skill. If you know how to learn, there are no limits to what you can do. It's more than just knowing how—it's about an intentional decision to make active learning a part of your way of life. Learning impacts your quality of life with a sharper mind, better mental health, and best of all, confidence. Learning is your most powerful weapon against imposter syndrome.

Here are some skills that support learning:

**1) Memorize.** When I was a young student, I went to a private Christian school. Each month I was required to memorize an entire chapter of scripture and recite it in front of the school. The longer I attended, the more I memorized and the easier it became. As a teenager I waited tables and never had to write down an order. Your brain is a muscle and performs at a high level when given the right kind of workout. Technology keeps track of everything from directions to phone numbers. You literally don't have to remember anything—and that is not good for our brains.

You can practice memorization by learning a poem or song. Try studying your grocery list and not referencing it until you think you are done. Learn techniques for remembering names before you attend the next networking event.

**2) Take notes.** When I was in school, we wrote down everything with a pen or pencil. I still have the callus on my finger from holding the pencil. We took notes during church, we wrote letters to pen pals, we kept diaries and journals and hand-drafted book reports and research papers. Studies have shown writing something down compared to typing improves retention. My keyboarding skills are strong. I can type as fast as I can think. I don't have to think as hard when I'm typing versus writing. When I write, I have to slow my thoughts down and intentionally think about the words I'm using and how to spell them. If you want to increase your retention, write stuff down.

**3) Chill out.** Most of us are living busy and stressful lives. Studies show that stress impairs learning and memory retrieval. Treat your brain like a sugar-amped toddler in need of a nap and give it a restorative break! Meditation, bubble baths, walks—whatever gives you the space to take a deep breath and restore your chill. And don't underestimate the benefits of a power nap. Studies show that a 45-minute nap results in five times better memory retrieval.

**4) Find your noise.** When I was homeschooling, I noticed how differently each child learned. Some needed to be away from distractions and noise. Others benefited from headphones playing wordless music to help them concentrate. Know yourself. Me? I need absolute quieter-than-the-library silence in order to focus. My husband does his work reports on the sofa with music in his earphones and the TV blaring. Clearly, he's a psychopath.

**5) Be the teacher.** A brain shift happens when you learn to teach. Instead of merely trying to pass a test, you are learning with the intent of mastery and retention. If you approach learning with the goal of being able to explain the process to a five-year old, you will retain more. Of course, there are many ways to share your knowledge with others, from starting a podcast, writing a book or launching a YouTube channel, to name a few. And why not? You have something amazing to share, so go ahead and put it out into the world.

With new ways to increase your learning skills, consider a learning "bucket" list. You are probably familiar with the bucket list concept as a way to list things you want to DO before you die. Well, this is your learning bucket list—the things you want to LEARN before you die. By writing down your list, you will be much more likely to take the time and effort to learn it. Once you have your list, set a time deadline.

## SKILL #2 - BRAINSTORMING

Brainstorming is one of my favorite activities. It taps into my creativity and innovation and feels like a competitive process. Our marketing agency uses brainstorming sessions to navigate rebranding projects, build SaaS or website platforms, sketch a course outline and more. Brainstorming is a skill that brings out the best ideas for our clients.

I have also used brainstorming techniques with my children to help lead them to a solution for their problems. I may or may not have used this technique on my husband too, but in case he reads the book, I'm admitting nothing. It is better we let him think it was all his idea.

Women's brains are wired in a way where we think about many different things at once. It's another of our awesome superpowers. The problem with having too many things swirling around in your head is that it becomes difficult to separate and categorize.

Brainstorming narrows your focus on a particular topic allowing you to "download" your ideas into a visual representation. By creating something visual you can build on your initial ideas. The visualization process leads to true innovation.

**The Four Rules for Brainstorming.**

Before you get started, there are rules to keep you on the right track.

1. **Focus on QUANTITY, not quality**. The goal of brainstorming is not to qualify an idea, but rather to encourage creativity. If you stop the process to qualify, you will spend all your time deciding if an idea has merit. Letting the ideas flow freely will allow ideas to build on themselves. Critical thinking comes later.

2. **No criticism!** When brainstorming with a group, you

want to encourage participation. If ideas are criticized, people will shut down.

3. **Encourage wild and crazy ideas.** Sometimes participation increases when a group is asked for their wildest and craziest ideas. I once facilitated a group of librarians on the development of their five-year strategic plan. The session opened with a challenge to come up with their craziest ideas for increasing visitors—even ideas they knew would never be approved. The resulting ideas included a live petting zoo in the children's area, trampolines embedded in the floor and a "Library Naked Day." The visual of both trampolines and naked people bouncing around had everyone howling. The ice breaker created an open-minded environment, not to mention the creative juices were now flowing.

4. **Combine and improve on ideas.** The best ideas do not usually materialize in a single thought. In my experience, the best ideas come when combined, evolved and built on. Building on ideas can only happen when participants feel valued and safe from criticism.

### Five Strategies to Successful Brainstorming

Some of these strategies will apply to a group setting and some for both individual and group brainstorming sessions.

1. **Know your objectives**. The cliché is true. If you do not know where you are going, you will never get there. Before you begin any brainstorming process, you need to know

what you hope to accomplish. In the case of the library, our objective was to determine how the library was or was not meeting community needs. Our objective gave us the destination around which we could design our prompts, activities and questions.

2. **Elect a facilitator.** The boss should never be the facilitator. Either get someone on your team to lead the brainstorming session or hire a professional. Nothing stifles creativity more than fearing your boss will think your ideas are dumb.

3. **Don't settle for average or safe.** You might be tempted to grab the first reasonably good idea and run with it. Don't do it. The amazing game changer idea is right around the corner if you hang in there. Keep building on, pulling apart and reassembling your idea until you tap into something great.

You can remove barriers with the question, "If time, money and resources were no object, how would we solve this problem?"

People often keep silent on ideas they do not think are possible and stick to ideas they feel will be accepted by the group.

4. **Keep order in the process.** Everyone deserves to have their ideas heard. If everyone is talking at once, it becomes impossible to collaborate on ideas. We have a large family and at Christmas we like to open one gift at a time. This past year my stepson's new girlfriend did not get the memo and

as the appointed "Santa" she had gifts flying everywhere. I still don't know what half of the gifts were. The same goes for brainstorming. Keeping order in the process will be more productive and keep good ideas from getting lost.

5. **Avoid anchoring**. Anchoring is a bias where our brains connect too heavily with the first idea we hear, similar to getting a song stuck in your head. To avoid anchoring while brainstorming, limit how much time is spent on a single idea. Get lots of ideas out before drilling down on any one of them.

A technique to help avoid anchoring is to have the participants write down their answers confidentially. The facilitator then writes them on a board for all to see. Anonymity keeps the individuals from judging their idea against ones already presented and results in a larger pool of ideas. Surveys also add the benefit of showing trends, if part of your objectives.

**Mind-mapping**

Mind-mapping is a common brainstorming technique and is a visual way to organize information. The map shows the relationships among different pieces of the whole. A mind-map works like the branches on a tree. There are ideas and then sub-ideas which branch off them. Mind-mapping is particularly useful for a process-driven problem or to find all the elements associated with an issue.

**Mind mapping basics**
- Central Theme: Your mind-map's central idea or problem will be in the center of a blank page.
- Associations: Draw a line out to another circle which represents a first level association.
- Supporting Information: Add key words that support the associations. Some tips to consider while mind-mapping:
  - Use key words. Keep it short and concise.
  - Use color and images! Studies show that those who use color and images when they are learning are more apt to remember.

While mind-mapping is often used as a solo technique, it can also be an effective tool in a small team environment. My agency team often uses mind-mapping as a tool for brainstorming structures and content for websites and online platforms. It gives us a visual of the user experience and later provides a "map" for us to follow when developing content. On the following page is an example of a mind-map built around Content Marketing Ideas.

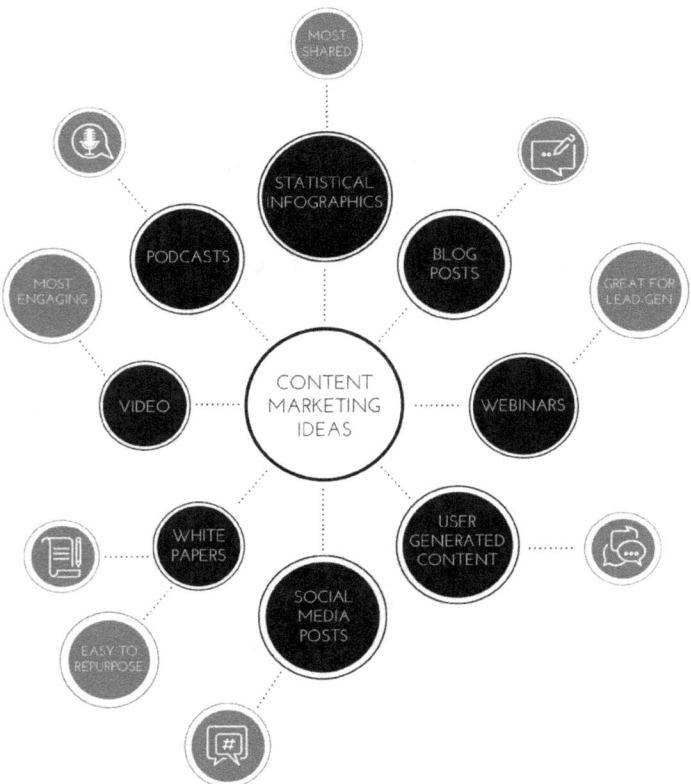

**The Post-It® Method.**

When it comes to brainstorming solo, Post-it® notes are your friend. These colorful blank squares are ideal for ideas to be written on, sorted and organized.

Before we dive in, I want to point out a few quick tips:
- Find a big blank wall, window or white board to work on.

- Try doing steps 1, 5 and 6 while standing up. Standing will help keep you focused and on-task. The physical part of being on your feet will help you remember as well. There is no science supporting this—or maybe there is—either way, trust me on the technique.

**STEP 1 – The Brain Dump**

When approaching a new problem or challenge, the first step involves a brain dump. A brain dump process allows you to clear your mind of ideas in the "low-hanging fruit" category. Set a timer for two minutes and then write down one idea per Post-it® as fast as you can. Stick them on the wall in a big, unorganized cluster. You will work on organizing them later.

**STEP 2 – Google**

Now, let's do some research on your problem or challenge. Google the phrase "Ways to [insert problem or challenge]" or "How do you [problem or challenge]." You will likely find a list of articles and blogs that have potential solutions you can add to your wall. Put each idea you find on a Post-it® note and add it to the wall.

**STEP 3 – Amazon Books**

Research is not done yet! Now go to amazon.com and type in the key words for your problem or challenge and search for books on the topic. Click on each relevant title and view the Table of Contents. Look for chapter headings which include ideas or possible solutions you can use. Write those down on Post-it® notes and add to the wall.

**STEP 4 – Online Courses**
There's one more place to dig for ideas. Visit udemy.com and search for online courses on the topic of your problem or challenge. Click on the course and review the "What You'll Learn" section. Write down any ideas you find on your Post-it® notes and add to the wall.

**STEP 5 – Organize Ideas**
By now you should have a pretty good collection of Post-it® notes stuck to your wall. Now you need to figure out how to organize all this information so it best serves the pursuit of ideas. Look at your notes. Do you see any ideas naturally grouping together? Rearrange the notes until groups or categories become apparent to you. Don't overthink it. You can—and probably will—change it later.

If you are stuck on how to categorize, you may need to do a quick mind map so you can visualize more clearly. Place them together in a group from left to right across the wall. If you think of a new idea, write it on a new Post-it® and place in a group. If you think of something that is not an idea on its own, but enhances another idea, write it on that Post-it®.

Whatever you do, don't overthink it. You can't do this wrong. You're just thinking here.

**STEP 6 – Prioritize your ideas**
Grab Post-it® notes in a different color and write the group or

category name and place at the top of each note cluster. Now tackle each group, one at a time. Perform a quick analysis of the idea and place the notes in order of priority beginning at the top. If there are a lot of ideas in one category, you may need to divide the category into a subset, or you can grade each idea by writing A, B or C on each. Put all the A's at the top, B's in the middle and C's at the bottom.

If there is something that ranks below a C in priority, reach out and snatch it off the wall. You do not need that kind of negativity in your life.

**STEP 7 – Record and transfer**
First things first. Take a picture. You will thank me later if something goes missing. If you are old school, you can transfer the Post-it® notes to a flip chart. If you do not have a flip chart, regular paper will work.

If you are comfortable with a digital option, get a free Trello.com account. Put your categories in the List Name and then each Post-it® below becomes a card under that column. Once in Trello, you will be able to easily move things around, add more ideas, keep track of links to resources and more.

Like any other skill or technique, it takes practice to achieve mastery. The art of brainstorming will serve you well. Next time you need to think through an idea or process, pull out brainstorming from your list of mompreneur superpowers.

*Having a plan doesn't mean being rigid and beholden to an unchanging plan. Planning means you know where you want to go and have thought through the process of getting there.*

### SKILL #3 - PLANNING

Most business owners do not have business or marketing plans. Perhaps they think it's too difficult. Or maybe they don't see the value in the effort. The problem with not having a plan is *you don't have a freaking plan*! You are vulnerable to falling down rabbit holes.

The discipline of planning is like installing guardrails for your entrepreneurial journey. When you fall asleep at the wheel, the plan will bump you back to your lane (and hopefully wake you up!). It also gives you the power of "no" to all the sales reps who come calling on your business. "I'm sorry. We've already made our plan for this quarter."

The process of planning IS a skill. You can learn how to do it and do it well. In business you will need plans for marketing, business, operations and more.

As a mom, you are making 3,214 different plans for your family. As you put planning in place, things in your world will run more efficiently and you will achieve established goals more often.

Regardless of the type of plan you need to create, these basic six steps are a good process for planning.

Step 1: Always determine your goals and objectives first.

Step 2: Create a time deadline for each milestone in your plan.

Step 3: Identify who is involved in making the plan happen.

Step 4: Prioritize all the action steps.

Step 5: Get feedback and consider alternative approaches.

Step 6: Factor in contingencies for the worst-case scenario.

Now, some of you are thinking, "I don't like to plan out every detail of my life." Then don't! Having a plan doesn't mean being rigid and beholden to an unchanging plan. Planning means you know where you want to go and have thought through the process of getting there.

## SKILL #4 - LEADERSHIP

Some may assume that leadership is a skill you either have or you don't. However, most great leaders do not come by their leadership abilities naturally. They learn the art of leadership and you can too!

In fact, as a mom you already possess the necessary traits of effective leadership. You are a manager, you adapt to an ever-changing environment and you are compassionate. The last one is often missing from many leaders today.

There are SO many books on the topic of leadership. Go read one—or 20. You'll find the overriding theme of being a great leader is not about being the bossy head honcho (unlike my first day of Kindergarten). Leadership is about serving and being a part of a team.

In the next chapter, we will keep the focus on leadership with Leadership Qualities of a Successful Mompreneur.

*Chapter 6*

# Leadership Qualities of a Successful Mompreneur

Being a mompreneur means being a leader. You are a leader to your kids. You are a leader in your business. You are a leader in your community.

There are four leadership qualities that have helped me on my journey:

**Know when to ask for help.**
It has always been difficult for me to accept help from others. I spent much of my adult life trying to prove myself by overachieving. It felt like weakness and weakness was never an option. In February 2015, our family home was destroyed in a fire. One minute we were sitting on the sofa researching spring break options on our laptops and five minutes later we were standing on the road watching flames take over our home.

The first act of kindness came while still standing on

*Sometimes remaining in a place of ideal margin means allowing others to bless you with some support.*

the street. A neighbor came by and slipped a $100 bill into my hand. I stared at the money. I stared at the neighbor. I was confused. Why did they give me money? People started calling. "What do you need?" they would ask. I didn't know how to answer the question. I would mumble "We're fine, really." Five days after the fire someone I had only met once called and asked, "What can I do?" By then I was overwhelmed by calls and random clothing donations in mysterious garbage bags. I blurted out, "I need someone to manage the calls and donations." She stepped up and allowed me the time to focus on loving my family as we navigated the next few weeks.

Here's a newsflash! You can be strong AND ask for help from your support network. Running a business while raising your kids is hard work. Sometimes remaining in a place of ideal margin means allowing others to bless you with some support.

Take support when it's offered. Ask for a helping hand when you need assistance.

**Create boundaries.** Raise your hand if it's important you ensure everyone around you is happy. Yep, me too. It's the mom gene. However, seeking to please others can become unhealthy when we allow ourselves to be stretched too thin by being too focused on everyone else. Boundaries are needed to avoid burnout and ensure others respect our time. The better you take care of yourself, the better you are able to serve others. Having the right boundaries in place is a great start.

Let me see a show of hands of those in denial and believe they already have strong boundaries in place. I see you, mama. You are doing "all the things" like a rock star. But if you're being really honest, you overcommit. We all do it. When you are trying to do everything, it's hard to do anything with excellence. Every day you complain about being tired and not having enough energy. Then you say yes to baking cupcakes until 2 a.m. for a bake sale when you could have said no. Sometimes you look at your kids or a client with resentment for demanding your time. Can I get a witness?

When it comes to boundaries, no one can decide what's truly important for your family or your business but you. You have a unique set of values, priorities and moving parts to your life.

Here are a few simple questions to help determine what boundaries might make sense for you:

1. **Ask yourself each morning, "What do I need today?"** Think about what you have on the calendar for the kids or commitments to clients. What needs to change? Do you

have the time, energy and bandwidth for everything? Do you need to ask for help? Are you taking care of your own well-being?

2. **Do you know how many clients is ideal?** Where are you in comparison to the number? What about your kids' activities? Are they doing too much?

3. If I operated using the 80/20 principle, or the "day before vacation" mindset, **what would I remove from my day?**

4. **Can you learn to say no?** No to working outside of your set schedule. No to anything that does not meet your priority standard. No to baking cupcakes at 2 a.m. No to more clients when you're already maxed out. No to letting people take you to lunch for free advice. No to more activities for the kids that don't align with your parenting objectives. **No is an empowering word.** Get comfortable with no and see how it can transform your world.

**Learn intentionally.** Leaders learn something new every day. They read or listen to books and podcasts or take courses when they identify a skill they need. The world is changing faster than ever before. You either become an intentional lifelong learner or accept you'll be left behind. Consider learning the best investment you'll ever make in yourself.

The coaching world has exploded because people are learning the value of support. If getting a business coach is not in your budget, consider a mastermind group like the Time to Thrive Membership (www.timetothrive.zone). [Shameless plug for which I'm not ashamed.]

**Give grace.** A mompreneur leader knows no one is perfect. Mistakes happen. We learn and we move on. Brace yourself for this little tidbit, ladies. THIS APPLIES TO YOU. Somehow, we think we are supposed to be in control of RESULTS. But we're not. We can control many things, but results are not one of them. Yes, of course we can TRY and do everything right to achieve a result, but there are factors beyond our control.

Mom guilt is real, and it sucks. We teach, coach, encourage, even require and your kids can still choose the wrong thing. And sometimes it's in a big public way. Ugh!

My middle daughter was 10 years old when I became her mama. She was defiant and stubborn and I instantly connected to her over our shared traits. She was like me in so many ways. I had enrolled all five kids in a homeschooling horseback riding class. We pulled into the parking lot in our Suburban, parking amidst all the minivans and SUVs. The families in attendance were from our church—so sweet and perfect in every way. Perfect bows decorated sweet little girl heads. Clean little boys with their hair slicked to the side. And then there was my crazy crew. Seriously, I considered it a win we arrived on time and everyone had on shoes.

Already I was feeling the mom guilt. After all, none of my girls had hair bows. I made a mental note on the hair bows for next time and we proceeded to the horse barn. Somewhere there was a beehive. There were bees everywhere, y'all.

*The Juggle is Real*

# *Grace is even more beautiful when we share it.*

It was like Armageddon. The kids bolted in a panicked run. My oldest daughter made it to the car first, which would have been fine had she not locked all the doors. My 10-year daughter got to the car shortly after her. Realizing her sister had locked her out, she stepped back and screamed, "You b****!"

The world went into slow motion.

Every God-fearing homeschooling mama stopped and turned for the source of THE word which assaulted their kids' ears.

When they located my crazed daughter, they slowly turned to look at me. I was standing frozen in place with my mouth hanging open in a silent prayer for God to take me right there. When I passed those ladies at church, I was sure they were referring to me as "the lady whose kid yells bad words."

Mom guilt.

Here's the thing. Did I deserve to feel guilty for something my kid did? Embarrassed, totally. But not guilty. You know why? Because I'm a good mom doing my best out here. My kids are not perfect. I'm not perfect. You're not perfect.

Next time you see a mortified mom waiting for the

earth to swallow her, give her a hug. Share a story of when you felt the same and have a good laugh together. Grace is even more beautiful when we share it.

You know the moment when you're talking with someone, and they completely change the subject without warning. This is your warning.

In the next chapter, we are going to dig into one of the most important aspects of a successful business.

*The Juggle is Real*

*Chapter 7*

# A successful business starts with a powerful brand

If I had to pick the one aspect of a business having the single most impact on its success, it would be brand. And let me clarify, I'm not talking about your logo. While creative assets are a reflection of your brand, they are not a brand by themselves. A brand should be considered one of the most valuable assets you can have as a company, the foundation through which everything else gets filtered.

Brand is defined as an individual's perception of a product, service, experience or organization.

Consider the benefits of a sniper rifle versus a shotgun. With a shotgun, you point in a general direction and shoot. Chances are good some of your shots will hit the target, but not all of them. Or you can fire a sniper rifle and hit what you're aiming at with much less work and from further distances away. If your goal is to hit the target, wouldn't you rather be working with a sniper rifle?

*Brand is defined as an individual's perception of a product, service, experience or organization.*

If I had to pick the one aspect of a business that has the single greatest impact on its success, it would be brand. The business world is a noisy and crowded place. Your brand identity is a special "thing" to help you stand apart.

- Uber isn't just a car service, it's "evolving the way the world moves."
- Airbnb isn't just a place to stay, it's "a trusted community marketplace for consumers to list, discover and book unique accommodations for unique travel experiences."
- Chipotle isn't just a restaurant, it's "bringing elements of fine dining to quick-service restaurants while seeking to cultivate a better world with respect for animals, farms and the environment."
- GoPro isn't just a camera, it's "enabling people to share their life through incredible photos and videos."
- AND YOU are not "just" a small business. Brand is about learning how to tell your story and why your story matters.

Volvo was founded on the concept of safety in 1927 in Gothenburg, Sweden. The company has a headline on their website, "There's more to Volvo than cars." The tagline is "Experience Volvo." The narrative includes the line, "We are a company that always puts people first."

In its ads, Volvo tells its brand story through powerful, relatable experiences the target audience understands—nothing is more important to a mother than the safety of her child. Search for one of their ads on YouTube and you'll see what I'm talking about. Volvo very effectively uses its brand to communicate a Volvo isn't "just a car," it's an investment in the safety of your family and others on the road. And who can put a price on that?

**Six reasons why brand drives success**

1. Presents a common face to the community
2. Creates a trusted familiarity to your name
3. Increases the perceived value of your product or service
4. Reinforces a competitive difference
5. Helps you gain a clear position and focus in your communications
6. Highlights a sense of purpose in what you do

A powerful brand will outline the promise you are making to your customers. Brand drives the perception you want your customers to have of your company. Ultimately, brand is your identity and becomes a part of your culture.

Customers have certain expectations when they interact with your business. Creating experiences which exceed expectations is what will create a memorable brand.

To be powerful and effective, a brand will have each of the following:

1. **Strategy**. A great brand is crafted through a deliberate process intentionally considering how to move a customer from having no awareness to becoming a raving fan. Brand strategy must be flexible enough to evolve and mature, as well as adapt to a changing marketplace.

2. **Passion**. Passion is contagious. If you have a genuine passion for your brand, it will show and others will catch it. Don't be afraid to give your brand transparency so your customers understand why you are so passionate about serving them.

3. **Relevant**. If it doesn't solve a problem for your customers, it doesn't matter. Why would it? Relevancy sparks interest and curiosity and moves a customer through your funnel. Taking the time to understand WHO your ideal customer is and what their pain points are will make all the difference in results.

4. **Adds value**. A great brand goes above and beyond. A leader in its industry, an influencer of trends, the value does not just meet expectations, but surprises and delights in unexpected ways. Value is more than competitive. Value is next level.

**The ideal customer.**

About 10 years ago, I was teaching a workshop to a group of small business owners at a local library. There were more than 100 people in attendance that day, which to be honest was the largest group I had ever spoken to up to that point. I was hyperventilating just a bit. But I digress.

I asked for a volunteer to describe their ideal customer. She confidently told me "everyone" was her ideal customer. She explained how her business made and sold handcrafted organic soap. Since "everyone" uses soap, "everyone" was her ideal customer. She was dead wrong.

Small business owners resist carving out a niche. The fear is we'll miss out on customers because we are ignoring them and focusing on a smaller group. What my soap-making entrepreneur had not considered is "everyone" is not willing to pay $5 for a bar of soap. Nor does "everyone" care if it's handcrafted and organic. However, there is a niche group of soap users who will pay $5 and who will care it's handcrafted and organic. And she needs to target THEM.

A few months ago, I had a coaching session with one of our Time to Thrive members. We brainstormed her ideal customer, their pain points and how she could create messages which would resonate with them. She went home and told a family member, who convinced her that was crazy because "everyone" can use her product. Ack!

Even if they CAN use your product or service, only your ideal customer WILL.

We can now agree that "everyone" is not your ideal customer. Your ideal customer is the one for whom you can solve a pain point in the MOST powerful way—and better than anyone else.

Describe individual buyer personas for potential customers in your target audience. Include a description of their age, gender, occupation, location, etc., so your marketing efforts will speak to them. Now, write offers to speak to their pain points and share how you can solve them. Include social proof from others in the same buyer persona segment.

Can you have more than one buyer persona? Absolutely. But usually, the wiser option is to start with one. Dial in and get it right before adding more segments. Get feedback. Tweak your message and process. When you have your marketing humming along, you can focus on the next buyer persona.

**Elements of your brand narrative.**
A brand narrative is made up of different elements. Each element provides a different perspective on your brand identity. They work together to consistently portray the desired perception in the mind of your ideal customer.

**Brand Personality.** Sometimes referred to as an elevator speech, since you have roughly 20 seconds on an elevator ride to answer the question, "What do you do?"

I like having a long and short version of the brand personality to use in different ways. The short version is the first sentence of the long version and concisely states what you do and why you do it.

Remember the four examples I shared at the beginning of this chapter?

Uber: "We are a car service company that is evolving the way the world moves."

Airbnb: "We are a trusted community marketplace for consumers to list, discover and book unique accommodations for unique travel experiences."

Chipotle: "We are bringing elements of fine dining to quick-service restaurants while seeking to cultivate a better world with respect for animals, farms and the environment."

GoPro: "We are a camera company that is enabling people to share their life through incredible photos and videos."

Now, you try drafting your short version by filling in the blanks:

We are (describe who you are / what you do) who (believes, develops, builds, etc.) + (your solution).

Once satisfied you have hit the mark with your short brand personality statement, add two or three sentences to expand. Be sure to include your approach, expected results of your product or service and how you solve their specific problem.

**Brand Focus**. These are three to five statements sharing the things you feel are truly important, what you focus on as a company and why it should matter to the customer.

Drafting your brand focus is about thinking through three or more results or actions you think about as the business owner all the time. For example, if creative custom solutions are in your top three desired results, include as a brand focus. For example: *We focus on creative solutions because the status quo won't move anyone forward.*

Your turn!

1. We focus on…
2. We focus on…
3. We focus on…

**Brand Process.** Laying out your "process" in a 1–2–3, step-by-step kind of way helps establish expectations, and reassures them you have a plan for how to work with them.

For example, your process might look something like this:

1. First, we ask questions. We know you have unique needs and we want to understand them.
2. Then we'll do our homework. We'll research and propose the best custom solution for your particular needs.
3. Finally, we'll share our recommendations and explain how we help you achieve your goals.

Can you see the benefit of communicating a brand process? It can be a part of your website, marketing collateral or even become a social media series.

**Brand Morals.** The vocabulary words you repeat most often reflect your inner values as an individual. The same is true for your brand identity.

Step #1—Imagine you are a fly on the wall listening to some customers who are talking about your business. What adjectives do you hope they would use? Write down between five and 20 words.

Step #2—Now go to thesaurus.com and enter each word to get a list of synonyms. Is there a different word that says it better? Is there a word with more depth or is more on target to your intent?

Step #3—Finalize your list and read the words out loud. Do they sound right in your ears? Make sure the words are genuine and you didn't pick them out because it was a cool word.

**Creative Elements.** There are six elements used to represent your brand identity. Each of these play a role in communicating your brand. It's important to ensure they align with your actual brand, or your customers may get confused about who you are.

**Logo.** A creative element most people are familiar with, but also tend to overthink, is the logo. The most successful brands have the simplest logos—think Apple, Target, Nike, etc. It's a mistake to try and make your logo "say" everything about you. A single image can only do so much.

When developing a logo, think clean and simple. It should be easy to recognize even from a distance or in small sizes. The image is about capturing the "essence" of your brand identity. The purpose is to reflect or represent, not tell the entire story.

**Colors**. Your brand's color palette is a powerful element of your creative impact. Colors can have certain associations attached to them, relay a mood or feeling or are even connected to a style or era. For example, green might represent growth, money or agriculture. Red is often seen as aggressive, while blue is calming. Browns and yellows might say, "Welcome to the '70s," while bright neon colors reflect a '80s vibe.

Your graphic identity should include two to four colors primarily used as part of your creative. You can also select two to four colors for secondary or tertiary options. Imagine you are a painter. If you only had two colors to work with, the painting would be flat. Likewise, having extra colors in your palette provides depth and interest to your marketing.

Colors will set the tone and become a strong, recognizable element. If you've ever had to repaint a room because the "samurai blue" looked great in the store, but was not so great on the walls, you'll understand the word of caution. Don't pick colors because you like them. Choose color strategically because they accurately represent your brand and marry together well.

**Style and shapes**. A creative element many people don't think about when crafting their logo and other assets is style and shapes. Is your brand techie? Modern? Whimsical? Style matters and affects your approach to the shapes you use in your creative arsenal. Make sure your style is also aligned with your brand.

**Tag line**. You might be wondering why I'm including the tagline as part of the creative elements. The tagline needs to be treated like one. For many years, we included tag lines in the logo design. More recently, we are treating the tagline as a separate piece of art. It can go with the logo or placed elsewhere. It can be text, or it can be text in a design form.

When it comes to writing, the tagline should be one of the last things you develop. The tagline is as short as one or two words and, ideally, no longer than seven. Shorter is better and as concise as possible. Use as a quick one-liner to define your company.

Can you name the companies associated with these taglines?

Just do it.

A diamond is forever.

Think different.

I'm lovin' it.

Because you're worth it.

**Typeface or font.** Your brand typeface is similar to style by driving an impression. It should align with the brand and interact seamlessly with all your other creative elements. You will need to choose at least two different typefaces.

The heading typeface is used for headlines or to stylize something with an added flair. While you can choose a typeface with more "style," ensure it is easy to read.

The body typeface is used for text in the body of something. It is the one you will use the most and needs multiple versions for bold, italics, etc.

Sometimes a third typeface is selected for digital use. If the body typeface you want to use doesn't look good on a screen, you might select something similar to hold its visual value better when used online.

**Imagery.** This final creative element provides the setting for your other elements. The imagery might be a series of background images or include deconstructed pieces of your logo. For example, if your logo had a circle element in it, you might create circle-based images to be incorporated in your marketing.

**Brand touchpoints.**
Touchpoints are any areas where you create a perception in the mind of your customer. The three categories of touchpoints are interactions between:

- **Human** – the customer and you or a team member.
- **Product** – the customer and your product or

service.

- **System** – the customer and the company.

Here are some examples of what touchpoints look like:

**Human**: Customer calls, Employee greets, Email follow-up

**Product**: Photos of your product, Experience with service, Instructions for using

**System**: Automated telephone system, Return policy, Billing / Invoicing process

**Touchpoint mapping.**

Once you understand the touchpoints in your business, you can map them. A touchpoint map gives us a visual representation of experiences where you can elevate your brand.

For most companies, there are five steps in the customer journey:

1) **Awareness**—the stage in which the customer first learns about you.

2) **Appeal or Consideration**—the stage in which the customer understands what you offer and finds it compelling.

3) **Purchase** is about the Ask & Act—the stage in which the customer might connect with the company, ask questions and gather information. Ask when they are making a buying decision.

4) **Retention**—maintaining customers and selling them other products or services

5) **Advocacy**—your customers share their experience with others.

Throughout the customer journey, they are influenced and impacted by touchpoints. The process of identifying and mapping those touchpoints will be your key to creating raving fans.

**Brainstorm your touchpoints.**
Face a big empty whiteboard or blank wall. Write out the five steps of the customer journey across the top from left to right. Now use the Post-It® Method to brainstorm all the human, product and system touchpoints under each step of the customer journey. Use a different color sticky note for human, product and system to visually see the categories. Encourage your team to participate and add touchpoints as they think of them.

Don't have a physical space? Use Trello.com to create a digital one and share with your team to collaborate.

**Map your touchpoints.**
Now that you have identified all your touchpoints, you can record them on a touchpoint map. Mapping touchpoints is a valuable tool for determining which touchpoints will help turn your customers into raving fans.

On the following page you'll find an illustration of a touchpoint map as a wheel. You can Google touchpoint

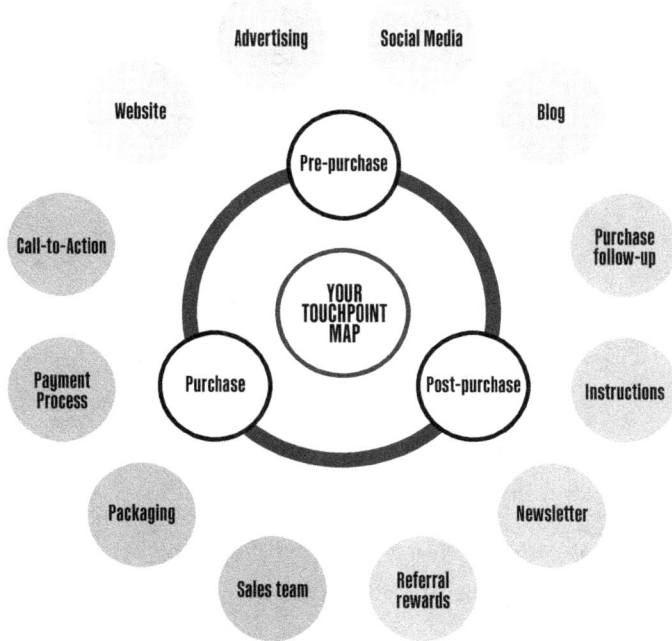

maps to see other configurations as well. Regardless of the way you design your touchpoint map, congratulate yourself on getting it done.

**Elevate your touchpoints.**
This is the part of the process where you decide how to best wow, surprise and delight your customers. Your customers expect performance on the big things based on their idea of the industry "standard." Where you can really make an impact is small actions that take them by surprise. Because they weren't expecting the action and because expectations

are exceeded, it is memorable. And when something is memorable, people talk to others.

Here are few ideas to get your creative juices flowing:

- Human Touchpoint | New Customer—send a handwritten thank you note
- Product Touchpoint | Receives Product—in the instructions include a link to a video SHOWING them step-by-step how to assemble
- System Touchpoint | Invoicing—include additional payment options so the customer can choose what's best for them—payment link, pay portal on website, send a check, call and pay, etc.

As you systematically work through your touchpoint map, you will slowly elevate your customer's experience. Each effort will ensure you exceed expectations at every turn, increasing your business through powerful word-of-mouth advertising.

**Audit your touchpoints**

The final step of your touchpoint strategy is to regularly audit your touchpoint map.

1. Have you been performing each of the elevated touchpoints consistently and as intended?
2. Based on actual experience, should you revise or tweak any of those elevated touchpoints?
3. Are there any new touchpoints to elevate?

*Do you think the information in this chapter will be helpful to your business? If you're interested in learning these kinds of tactical and practical strategies for business growth, consider joining the Time to Thrive Membership.*
www.timetothrive.zone

*The Juggle is Real*

*Chapter 8*

# Smoothing out friction

As a mom and a business owner, most of your days run by like a blur. So many things, so little time. Am I right?

The idea of smoothing out friction has kept me sane during very stressful times and is a way of life I've embraced and serves me well. Because the tactic has been such a game-changer for me, I want to share it with you.

Think about the last time you were stuck in bumper-to-bumper traffic because of an accident. I mean super stuck. The longer you sit in traffic, the more aggravated you feel. You watch with annoyance as some yahoo creeps down the shoulder because his needs are more important than everyone else's. Ahh! It's stop-and-go, so you can't afford to take your eyes off the road or you'll end up tapping the bumper in front of you. You pull slightly over into the shoulder and strain your neck looking for the cause of the delay. You call your destination and let them know you'll be late because of traffic. You check your maps app and see the delay is going to be at least an hour. Suddenly you realize the extra large sweet tea you have been drinking was a bad idea. You start looking for a wooded area on the side of the freeway. Maybe no one will notice if you just slip behind a tree real quick.

Friction.

Our personal and business lives are full of friction. Things not operating as they should cost us productivity, time and peace of mind. Busy mamas have a habit of "dealing" with something in the moment because we don't have time to fix it.

- You tie your kid's shoe for the fourth time today and wish she'd learn to tie her shoes already.
- You're putting away groceries and notice you bought Italian seasoning and you already have three bottles—and two of them are expired.
- Your employee took a two-hour lunch for the third time this month. But you hate confrontation, so you put off the needed conversation.
- You can't find your keys, your glasses, your sanity. Where did I put my sanity again?
- Your kid announces at 9 p.m. they have a science project due tomorrow. For. The. Love.

Friction will rob you of your peace over and over.

## Smoothing out friction

The transition from having an only child to suddenly caring for five children is like drinking from a fire hose. It's overwhelming and daunting. One of the biggest adjustments for me was noise level. My only child didn't do a lot of yelling and screaming because there was no one to argue with. Add a few more children to the mix and the yelling and screaming were pretty much constant.

Friction.

Nothing would power up the yelling and screaming like everyone vying for "shotgun." Apparently when you're a preteen, sitting in the front seat of the car is the premium spot. The arguments over who was sitting shotgun were fierce. "I called it first!" "You had it last time." Ugh! Mama had enough and assigned seats. The oldest in the vehicle always gets shotgun and everyone else sits in their assigned seats. I know. I'm a monster. But the friction is gone.

I could tell you dozens of stories about how I had to reduce friction by taking some sort of action to solve it.

- Kids wearing socks outside with no shoes—what on earth? Solution: The culprit had to wash their socks by hand in the sink a few times. Friction gone.
- "Who left their wet towel on the floor?" "Not me!" And now I'm picking it up and grumbling about it. Solution: Color-coded towels for each kid and now I immediately knew who to call to come pick it up. Friction gone.

- Feeding all these kids all day every day was wearing me out. Solution: One big cooking day every six weeks and storing ready-made meals in the freezer. Friction gone.
- Kids sassing me. See my solution in Chapter 10. Friction (mostly) gone.

Same is the case for business. Clients who take more than what they pay for. Vendors underdelivering on promises. Printers always out of ink at the worst possible moment. An endless list of opportunities to smooth out the business journey.

Give a bit of thought to identifying friction. Then implement action, accountability, steps to avoid and reduce or solve it. Easier said than done, but isn't peace worth it?

Yes, it takes time and effort to solve friction. People will push back and complain (mostly your kids). Too bad for them. I chose not to live in a state of friction, and you don't have to either.

You also don't have to solve every point of friction in one day. It's a process, a way of life. It's about deciding you want to have calm and peace and being intentional about making it happen.

Life doesn't happen to you unless you let it. Decide what kind of life you want and then become the architect that builds it, one brick (i.e. moments of friction gone) at a time.

**It starts with awareness.**

You can't solve a problem until you know it exists. We walk through our day focused on getting everything done on the schedule. Unless we are open to it, we don't leave room for awareness. Instead, we are annoyed, but keep moving. Friction robs us of our peace, but we accept it as the way it will be.

Sometimes we have to get completely fed up with something before we act. Why do we do that? Wouldn't it be better if we addressed the issue the *first* time it gave us trouble? Instead, we're allowing ourselves to be annoyed and frustrated about the same thing over and over. I'm pretty sure we have identified the textbook definition of insanity.

What if we decided to focus on one piece of friction every day? That's 365 ways our lives would run smoother in one year! Too daunting? How about one piece of friction a week? That's still 52 things in a year contributing to a more peaceful life. Your peaceful life. My peaceful life.

**Solving friction.**
Dealing with friction is about progress, not perfection. Choosing a peaceful life does not mean we'll never have friction. It means we have the mindset and process in place to cut it off at the knees.

Let's choose one point of friction in your family life right now. What frustrates you on a regular basis? Now think about possible solutions.

When thinking about solutions, don't worry about whether your kids will agree or not agree. Their buy-in is not required. In fact, you should count on getting pushback.

Any change worthwhile will get pushback.

People, including your kids, don't like change. But change happens and YOU are the mama. YOU are the boss. YOU know what is best for your kids and your family, and sometimes it will make you unpopular for a hot minute. They will thank you later—maybe a lot later. But one day when they have kids, they will realize a peaceful life always requires change from chaos.

Once you have a solution, communicate it, stand by it, implement it and insist on it when necessary. We have a new procedure. No take backs. No discussion. No power struggles. You got this, mama.

**Here are some of the areas where I addressed friction to help you think about yours:**

- Making lunches was a chore I forgot about until the last minute and was left throwing random food items in a bag. (Trigger the mom guilt!) Some of you are out there cutting sandwiches into stars, and if that's you, I'd like to officially thank you for making me look bad [*sarcasm intended*]. My solution was to make lunches while I was cooking dinner. I was already in food prep mode so while I was waiting on something to cook, it was easy to put some lunches together. Even better, make an extra (regular or star-shaped) sandwich, and pack several days' worth of lunches at a time.

  - I'm a bit addicted to my phone. This amazing little

handheld device can do almost anything—and it does. As a result, it's perpetually running low on battery. If I don't have a charger where I need one, it's friction, people. Making sure chargers are in places where you need them lessens frustration. See how easy this is?

- With five children comes a lot of random stuff. The stuff seemed to fall off them somehow as they walked through the house. I couldn't keep track of who all the stuff belonged to, which also frustrated me. I came up with a lost and found. All random stuff, not where it was supposed to be, was collected each evening and put in lost and found. No announcement. No attempt at locating its owner. Just gone. When the owner of the item realized it was missing, they would ask me. To get it back, I required a written essay on being a good steward or how to accept personal responsibility. After an essay or two, random stuff was no longer an issue. Anything not claimed was donated as no one wanted it enough to write me an essay, therefore we didn't need it!

- We live on a lake and our family spends every Sunday in the good weather months enjoying it—which means lots of wet bathing suits, towels and random clothing items. These items used to end up everywhere—hanging over the deck rail, on a hook in the boat house, or horror of horrors, on my living room hardwood floors. It only took one Sunday of asking them to throw them in the washing machine instead. Now they automatically do this every Sunday and I add in the detergent and run the load. No one has to die for messing up my hardwood floors.

- We have a lot of spices and I didn't have an available cabinet to keep them all in. I decided to use the cabinet over the double oven. When making a recipe, I'd have to pull out a step stool to reach up in the cabinet. It was less than convenient. I finally got so fed up I searched Amazon for spice organizing solutions. I found a cheap option to go in a drawer and I went to work. I pulled out all the spices and put them in matching containers with cute labels. Now they are stored in the drawer under my stove top in alphabetical order. I swear I hear angels singing every time I open it—or maybe it's just me.

- After the successful spice drawer, I got a little excited about it and expanded my focus into the pantry, the laundry room, the linen closet, the master bedroom closet and bathroom cabinets. It's addictive. And, whatever you do, don't binge watch *The Home Edit* unless you want the addiction too. You've been warned.

There you have it! The secret to a more peaceful life starts with removing one piece of friction, then another, and then another. When life runs smoothly, you have more margin on your time and energy.

*Chapter 9*

# Establishing parenting objectives

For eleven years, I raised an only child. She was shy and very agreeable. She enjoyed reading and quietly played with her Barbie dolls for hours. She was easy to correct and submissive to my authority. During this time of parenting, there was zero thought given to the adult version of the child I was raising. After all, I was obviously killing this parenting thing and she was happy and healthy. Isn't that what matters?

As I prayed in the months leading up to the adoption of a sibling group of four children, I asked God to create the right environment to bond with my children. To my horror, the bonding opportunity manifested itself as a violent stomach bug.

The oldest came down with it first. We spent a solid six hours on the bathroom floor while he vomited over and over. I rubbed his back and put a cool cloth on his head and said all the reassuring things a mom can say.

The second oldest came down with it the next night. I heard her scream for me from her bedroom and I leapt out of bed. As I turned the corner to the hall, she was coming down the stairs and landed at the opposite end of the hall. The projectile vomit sprayed the hallway wall about two feet from her and extended another six feet or so down the hall. I watched as it slowly ran down the wall and said a silent thank you that I wasn't two seconds faster. Otherwise, I would have taken it square in the chest.

By the third night I was dizzy with exhaustion. As I'm tucking everyone in for the night, the youngest tells me her stomach hurt. Please, God, no! I brought her down to the living sofa and made her cozy with a bucket at the ready. I stumbled to bed. I felt myself sinking backwards into blackness when I heard something in the living room. When I got to her, I could see she had been sick in the bucket. I ask why she didn't call for me. She said she didn't want to bother me. Tears flowed down my face. Partly because I was exhausted, but also because no eight-year-old should be sick without knowing they can call their mom.

At the end of our first week, we all felt like we had gone through a war. However, our bond had begun and the seeds of family had been planted.

The experience opened my eyes to purpose behind everything we do as parents. I wasn't just taking care of sick children; I was showing them what love looks like. The kind of love that shows up when it's exhausting and involves being vomited on for three days. For children who had never experienced this kind of love before, it opened their eyes too.

The OTHER life lesson here is to be careful what you pray for. Just saying.

For the next six months, I spent many hours in my walk-in closet hiding—and let's get real for a minute, crying a lot of tears. Ok, it was more like sobbing and snot bubbles. I was struggling. I had doubts about my ability to be the best mom for these kids. What had I done? Why did I think I was equipped for being a mom to five children? They were noisy and messy and didn't listen to anything I said. Clearly, I was failing.

God gave me reminders I was equipped through my business experience. I dug into creating processes and systems, consistent boundaries and accountability. Who knew being a business owner was so much like being a mom!

Being a mompreneur is not about survival. It's about purpose.

**The first step.**

The first step to any problem is understanding what you want to happen. You start with your goals and then reverse engineer action steps to get you there.

It's nice to think about our kids being in the popular group or the athletic superstar. We want them to be liked by their peers and be happy. But what if we got past the short-term temporary "happiness?" What if we figured out what would make a difference in 10, 20 or 30 years? What if we focused on helping our children become who they need to be to live out their purpose?

Let that sink in for a minute. Yikes. No pressure, right?

**Developing parenting objectives.**
The amazing thing about individual families is their unique qualities. My family is different from your family. Your parenting objectives are going to reflect your values and beliefs, not mine.

I thought about the characteristics I wanted my kids to have as adults and decided on the following:

- A heart for serving and helping others
- Gratitude for our blessings and contentment with what we have
- Mercy and forgiveness as gifts to be shared generously
- Taking personal responsibility means accepting the consequences of your actions and not blaming others
- Work with excellence in everything you do

Take a moment and think about your parenting objectives. What does this look like for your family?

1.
2.
3.
4.
5.

Our first Christmas together did not go as planned. The adoption process took longer than expected and it was the end of February before we were able to bring them home. We decided to wait on Christmas. Two additional months gave me more time to accumulate a ridiculous pile of gifts. Not only did they not fit under the tree, but you could barely see the tree!

The next morning, they tore through gift after gift. At first, they were excited, but as the experience wore on, their enthusiasm began to wane.

If I had been clear on my parenting objectives (i.e. number two on my list), my actions would have reflected my goals. The next Christmas we started a new tradition. Baby Jesus received three gifts, so each child also received three gifts. We all watched as each gift was opened. Other family traditions were introduced we still do today. We shifted our focus from the number of gifts to teaching the reason for the season. Instead of the holiday being all about the kids, we baked cookies for neighbors. Instead of exhaustion from opening so many gifts, we celebrated each gift with a grateful heart. Now our Christmas was aligned with our parenting objectives.

**Making different choices.**

When you use your parenting objectives as a guide, you are able to make different choices for your family—choices which support and reflect your long-term goals for your children.

For example, if you want children who are:

- Grateful. Stop buying them every toy, gadget and gizmo.
- Confident. Stop doing everything for them. They can (and should) do it for themselves.
- Unselfish. Stop making them the center of the family's schedule and checkbook.
- Loving. Stop making it about them and give them opportunities to serve others.
- Independent. Stop rescuing them when they forget or make a mistake.

Think about the parenting objectives you decided on. What actions do you need to stop or start doing to ensure you are moving toward them?

Making different parenting choices is not always easy or convenient. I was shopping at a big box wholesale store with my daughter, who tended to take things without asking. The cashier did not notice the watermelon under the cart. We were in the parking lot and halfway to the car when my daughter notices the watermelon is not on our receipt. She was all excited about our "free watermelon!" I turned around and we went back in the store and stood in line for 30 minutes to pay for it. This exercise was not about the watermelon, but about teaching her the importance of honesty and integrity. I was teaching her we don't take things that don't belong to us. It wasn't convenient, but I was on a mission greater than convenience…or free watermelon.

**Teachable moments.**
My kids joked that I could turn anything into a "teachable moment," whether something went sideways, someone was mean or a mindset was off-base. Teachable moments are everywhere, but you must be willing to stop and invest in them.

Teachable moments are incredible opportunities to have conversations with your kids. By asking them questions and really getting an understanding of what is going on in their heads, you are better equipped to guide them.

- Why do you think that happened?
- What could you/they have done to get a different result?
- What were you/they feeling when they made that choice?
- Was that right or wrong? Why do you think that?

It's not about lecturing, it's about asking questions and actively listening. When you share your thoughts, they will hear you because you have shown you care about what they think and how they feel.

I do not always get this right. I get it wrong more than right. But when you get it right, it's pure magic.

*The Juggle is Real*

*Chapter 10*

# Creating a custom parenting plan

As I navigated my new role as mom of many, I worked out reward systems, consequence-based systems and hybrids of both. They all seemed so brilliant until I tried implementing them. Often, they were too complicated, resulting in no one being clear on the rules of engagement, me included. Other systems were too dependent on me to enforce them and they fell apart because I couldn't be consistent. I also realized that the adage, "Rome wasn't built in a day" is a saying for a reason.

I decided to focus on one thing at a time. Now that doesn't mean I didn't address other things. It meant I was only going to change the way I handled one thing at a time and be crazy consistent.

I embraced my new focus like my life depended on it. Failure could mean complete loss of sanity. That didn't seem like an appealing option.

The thing driving me craziest of all was disrespect in all its forms. There is nothing which will make me battier than getting into a circular argument with a child who has no reasoning or common sense whatsoever. You know it's fruitless while you're in the middle of it, yet you find yourself doing it over and over again. Ugh. And don't even get me started about how it makes me feel when a child rolls their eyes, lets out an exasperated sigh or throws out their hip and crosses their arms. To the moon with you!

I knew I was taking on the monster. The big one. The toughest behavior to change. I didn't care. I was desperate.

The new "system" I put together was the key to saving my life.

Saving my life might be a might dramatic, but it sure felt like it at the time. When I figured out something that worked, this is what happened.

- I stopped yelling to be heard.
- I stopped losing my **** like some sort of crazy person.
- I stopped feeling like a bad mom.
- I stopped participating in arguments with children.
- I stopped crying in my walk-in closet.

And you know what else happened?

- Disrespect was less of an issue.
- We enjoyed extended moments of peace and calm.
- Children were genuinely happy and secure.

- It made room for other areas of behavior to be addressed.
- Hope abounded that maybe, just maybe, I could, in fact, do this parenting thing.

**The Tickets**

As a mompreneur, I needed a disciplinary system where I could be consistent without getting overwhelmed. The "ticket system" became the framework for my parenting plan.

I believe it works so well because:

- Completely scalable - one child or ten children
- Adapts to any age
- Easy to enforce
- Simple for the kids to be clear on what is expected
- Works anywhere—at home or elsewhere
- Works regardless of the rules of the house

Sounds great, right? But that's not even the best part. The tickets reinforces every single one of the parenting objectives. Can you imagine? As you are disciplining and maintaining order, you are also building character, encouraging the right mindsets and supporting your parenting goals.

**The crucial elements of the tickets include:**

1) The rules of your home

2) Two warning phrases

3) The time-out option

4) The tickets themselves

**The Rules.**

The rules of your home should be age-appropriate and comprehensive enough to cover most situations. We used *The 21 Rules of This House* by Gregg Harris. You can search online for their coloring book and/or laminated sign to post on your fridge.

The 21 rules of our house were:

1. We obey God (by the way, this one rule covers a lot of ground).
2. We love, honor and pray for one another.
3. We tell the truth.
4. We consider one another's interests ahead of our own.
5. We speak quietly and respectfully with one another.
6. We do not hurt one another with unkind words or deeds.
7. When someone needs correction, we correct them in love.
8. When someone is sorry, we forgive them.
9. When someone is sad, we comfort them.

10. When someone is happy, we celebrate with them.
11. When we have something nice to share, we share it.
12. When we have work to do, we do it without complaining.
13. We take good care of everything God has given us.
14. We do not create unnecessary work for others (especially Mom).
15. When we open something, we close it.
16. When we take something out, we put it away.
17. When we turn something on, we turn it off.
18. When we make a mess, we clean it up.
19. When we do not know what to do, we ask.
20. When we go out, we act just as if we were in this house.
21. When we disobey or forget any of the 21 rules of this house, we accept the consequences.

Take what you like from the list and add your own rules or variations. Your house. Your rules. What's important is that you actually have a set of established rules communicated and posted in writing. Without rules, you can't be consistent.

**Warning Phrases.**

Kids are kids. They don't have a fully developed brain. They forget, get distracted and choose poorly. It's a mystery why we are continually surprised by this!

A warning phrase *empowers* them with the choice to

change behavior. If they choose not to change behavior, they will have to accept the consequences for the choice.

**BEWARE.** The entire system will break down if you get angry and flip the script into a threat instead of a warning. Saying, "Do it or else" is a threat. Or if you go beyond one warning and the boundary is not clear, you have caused a breakdown.

The same phrases should be used every time. My two warning phrases were "Would you like to rephrase that?" if it was verbal, or "Would you like to rethink that?" if it was behavior. Feel free to use my phrases or come up with phrases of your own.

You should not deviate from the warning phrase. Commit to it and use it the same way every single time.
The warning phrases are your proverbial line in the sand. You must hold the line, or you will lose credibility. Children push until they meet resistance. Your warning phrase is the resistance needed to let them know you are serious, and they now have a choice to make.

Be prepared for this line in the sand to be tested. Often.

**The time-out option.**
Sometimes situations got emotional. I would be upset and/or my kid was upset. It's hard to be respectful when emotions are high. I introduced the time-out option to give space to calm down before responding. Time outs applied to me as well as them.

If I felt I couldn't keep my cool, I'd call for a 10-minute

time-out to get myself together. If their emotions were running high, I'd ask if they wanted to do a 10-minute time-out.

The time-out option taught them not to react in the moment and to see the value in not making decisions until they had a cooler head.

Once the time-out was over, I'd return to the warning phrase and they would choose the response.

**The tickets**

Our "tickets" were a typed list of consequences I had cut into strips, folded them and put into a container. For the most part, consequences were chosen to support my parenting objectives.

Below is what I put on my tickets, but make your own list based on your parenting objectives.

- I looked up scripture verses which addressed each of my parenting objectives. Younger children can copy the verse while older kids can write it out 20 times and/or memorize it.

- Short essays on responsibility, serving and stewardship. Younger children can draw a picture that shows the concept until they can write at least 50 words. Older children can write 200 words or more.

- A list of chores serving the family as a whole, or someone specific in the family. I definitely included some chores to make my life easier, such as wiping down switch plates, dusting baseboards or organizing the pots and pans drawer.

- About 1 in 10 tickets were mercy tickets. It's exactly what it sounds like. A free pass. If you want to teach the concept of forgiveness and mercy, give them an opportunity to experience it. In the moment, they KNOW they should get a consequence, but they are given grace instead. What a beautiful lesson!

**The process.**
Putting the tickets into effect will change the entire temperature in your home. As a mompreneur, you don't have time for nagging, circular arguments about nothing or someone dancing on that one last frayed nerve.

It took us about two weeks before we settled into the process. From there, it got better and better with time. My house was more peaceful and my kids were happier. It's worth the investment to get this in place.

The process has the following steps:

1. You see or hear the behavior.
2. (Sometimes you give a time-out option.)
3. You give ONE warning phrase (and ONE ONLY).
4. If child does not comply, you say, "that's one ticket" and repeat warning phrase.
5. If child does not comply, you say, "that's two tickets" and repeat warning phrase.

You can remain calm and smile because you are just there to hold the line.

What if they refuse to do what's on the ticket?

Once a child has been given a ticket, all privileges are suspended until whatever is on the ticket is completed. All. Of. Them. No screens. No phones. No playing. No pool time. No soccer. No dance. No nothing.

If they are disrespectful at any point, you just calmly ask "Would you like to rephrase?" and smile. Always smile. Partly because it keeps you calm, but mostly because it really annoys them.

When they KNOW you are going to hold the line, they will stop pushing back, so hold the line! When you're tired, hold the line. When you're busy, hold the line. Nothing is more important than holding the line.

**Key hints to ensure you are successful.**

1. Only ONE warning, then give a consequence. This is essential for it to work.
2. Be consistent with your warning phrase. Whatever it is, always use it.
3. Don't forget to use the time-out option, if needed. Everyone needs to keep their cool.
4. Throw the tickets out once they've been pulled. Print off a new list once you run out.
5. Post your rules.
6. Never ever get sucked into an argument again. Behavior,

warning, consequences.

7. Smile. It helps keep you calm and loving, even when you don't feel like it.
8. Don't forget to praise them. There's always a reason to praise. Praise them for getting their self-control back quickly. Praise them for only one ticket instead of two like last time.
9. Never threaten with a ticket. Always use the warning phrase.

If you would like to go deeper into the topic of parenting, consider ordering my book *Getting a Grip,* available on Amazon.

*Chapter 11*

# Building a tribe

Nothing hurts a mama's heart more than your child feeling like they don't have any friends. That might explain why one of the most common "mom lines" of all time is, "you must be a friend to find a friend."

When was the last time you were a friend to someone you didn't know?

The idea of having an entire tribe of BFFs who love you unconditionally, want to see you succeed and who never ever stab you in the back is a nice thought. In the real world, most of us are truly blessed if we have one or two friends who truly know us—and love us because they think our crazy is awesome.

If I'm going to be truly honest with you, I have not been good BFF material. I struggle with the time needed to invest in relationships outside of my husband and family. And I've been hurt enough times by women I thought were friends to

## *Building a tribe requires effort because relationships do not just happen.*

be shy about putting myself in a vulnerable position again.

Building a tribe requires effort because relationships do not just happen.

The older I get, the more I seem to crave sisterhood. A few years back a friend hosted a weekend business retreat for women business owners. That weekend was transformational for me. I watched the spark light up in individuals as 16 other women cheered them on. We cried together. We laughed together. We bonded and it was a beautiful thing. I saw the difference a tribe can make.

Whether for a short time or for a lifetime, sisters (biological or not), make life better. To be successful as a mompreneur, having a community of women who understand the juggle is real is priceless.

You will know you have "sisterhood" community when:

1. **They are fierce protectors**. Everyone understands the concept of a mama bear and her cubs. Mess with a member of the sisterhood and the rest will come for you.

2. **They keep us in line**. When you have a true sister, she speaks truth into your life. And when necessary,

gives you a big ol' proverbial kick in the backside.
3. **They are your biggest cheerleaders**. Your sister tribe will cheer you on loud and proud. They show up to celebrate your wins and are an encouragement in between celebrations.
4. **They empower you to do more than what you can do alone**. When you are deeply connected to a tribe, you matter. What you think, do, feel and say matters. Living up to your potential matters. And so, you do.

Many of us have trouble being intentional about sisterhood because we've spent a good bit of our careers competing with men in business. Yep, I went there.

My first boss—a man. My first sales manager—a man. My first business partner—a man. I spent all my formative years reporting to and attempting to impress and earn respect from men in power positions. When I went to a networking event, I'd instinctively look for the "most important" men in the room—the ones I needed to meet to advance my business agenda.

If you were born after 1990, maybe this is less true for you. I'd like to think things have changed for women in business. Either way, being a part of a mompreneur sisterhood is a way to move us all forward in business.

**Creating a tribe of sisters.**
If you are ready to create a sisterhood, here's a few ideas to

help you start building your tribe.

1. **Be proactive**. Women, moms and especially mompreneurs are busy. Instead of waiting for women to reach out to you, be proactive in reaching out to them. Think about all the women you know from your past with whom you lost touch. Send them an email, drop a DM or make a phone call and reconnect with those you want to include in your tribe. Continue to nurture the relationships.

2. **Focus on women**. Next time you walk into a networking event, focus specifically on women you want to meet. Before you attend, identify two or three women you'd like to connect with and seek them out.

3. **Create opportunities**. Find opportunities to be around the ideal women you want to include in your tribe. I spent too many years with my head down thinking I didn't have time for "socializing" or "networking." Prioritize the time you spend investing in your tribe.

In today's digital world, there are more opportunities than ever to connect or get lost in a crowd. When you understand the value of having a tribe, you are more likely to be intentional about creating one.

---

My sweet friends, I'm so glad you decided to be a part of *The Juggle is Real*. I hope you found some wisdom in these pages you can use with your family and business. As we close our time together, remember you are amazing and you are doing a great job. Keep moving forward, leveling up and staying true to your purpose.

God bless.

www.ingramcontent.com/pod-product-compliance
Lightning Source LLC
Chambersburg PA
CBHW071126240526
45465CB00024B/1406